D1517494

■SCHOLASTIC

News

Nonfiction Readers

Math in the Kitchen

by Ellen Weiss

Children's Press®
A Division of Scholastic Inc.
New York Toronto London Auckland Sydney
Mexico City New Delhi Hong Kong
Danbury, Connecticut

These content vocabulary word builders are for grades 1–2.

Math Consultant: Linda K. Voges, EdD, Cohort Coordinator/Lecturer, College of Education, The University of Texas at Austin

Reading Consultant: Cecilia Minden-Cupp, PhD, Early Literacy Consultant and Author, Chapel Hill, North Carolina

Photographs © 2008: Bancroft Variel: back cover, 5 bottom, 5 top left, 11, 15, 21; Corbis Images Sharie Kennedy/LWA: cover; Getty Images/Dave & Les Jacobs: 7; PhotoEdit: 1, 5 top right, 12 (Laura Dwight), 9 (David Young-Wolff); StockFood, Inc./Johnson: 2, 4, 13, 17, 19.

Book Design: Simonsays Design!; Book Production: The Design Lab

Library of Congress Cataloging-in-Publication Data
Weiss, Ellen, 1949–
Math in the kitchen / by Ellen Weiss.
    p. cm.—(Scholastic news nonfiction readers)
Includes bibliographical references and index.
ISBN-13: 978-0-531-18531-5 (lib. bdg.)   978-0-531-18784-5 (pbk.)
ISBN-10: 0-531-18531-1 (lib. bdg.)   0-531-18784-5 (pbk.)
1. Mathematics—Juvenile literature. 2. Cookery—Juvenile literature. I. Title. II. Series.
QA40.5W4456 2008
510—dc22   2007005863

CONTENTS

WORD HUNT

Look for these words as you read. They will be in **bold**.

estimate
(**es**-tuh-mate)

measuring cup
(**meh**-zhu-ring kup)

2 x 2 = ?

multiply
(**muhl**-tuh-ply)

half cup
(haf kup)

measure
(**meh**-zhur)

quarter cup
(**kwor**-tur kup)

recipe
(**res**-uh-pee)

Now You're Cooking with Math!

We're going to have fun in the kitchen today.

Let's use math to make a yummy birthday cake.

Can you tell these kids are using math?
We use math often when we cook.

We are going to have a big birthday party.

Twelve people will be here!

But our **recipe** says the cake will serve only 6 people.

What should we do?

Always check the recipe to see how many people it will serve.

We'll just have to double the recipe.

To double means to **multiply** everything by 2.

That will make plenty of cake!

Look at the recipe.

It calls for 2 eggs.

If we double it, how many eggs will we need?

Turn to page 23 for the answer.

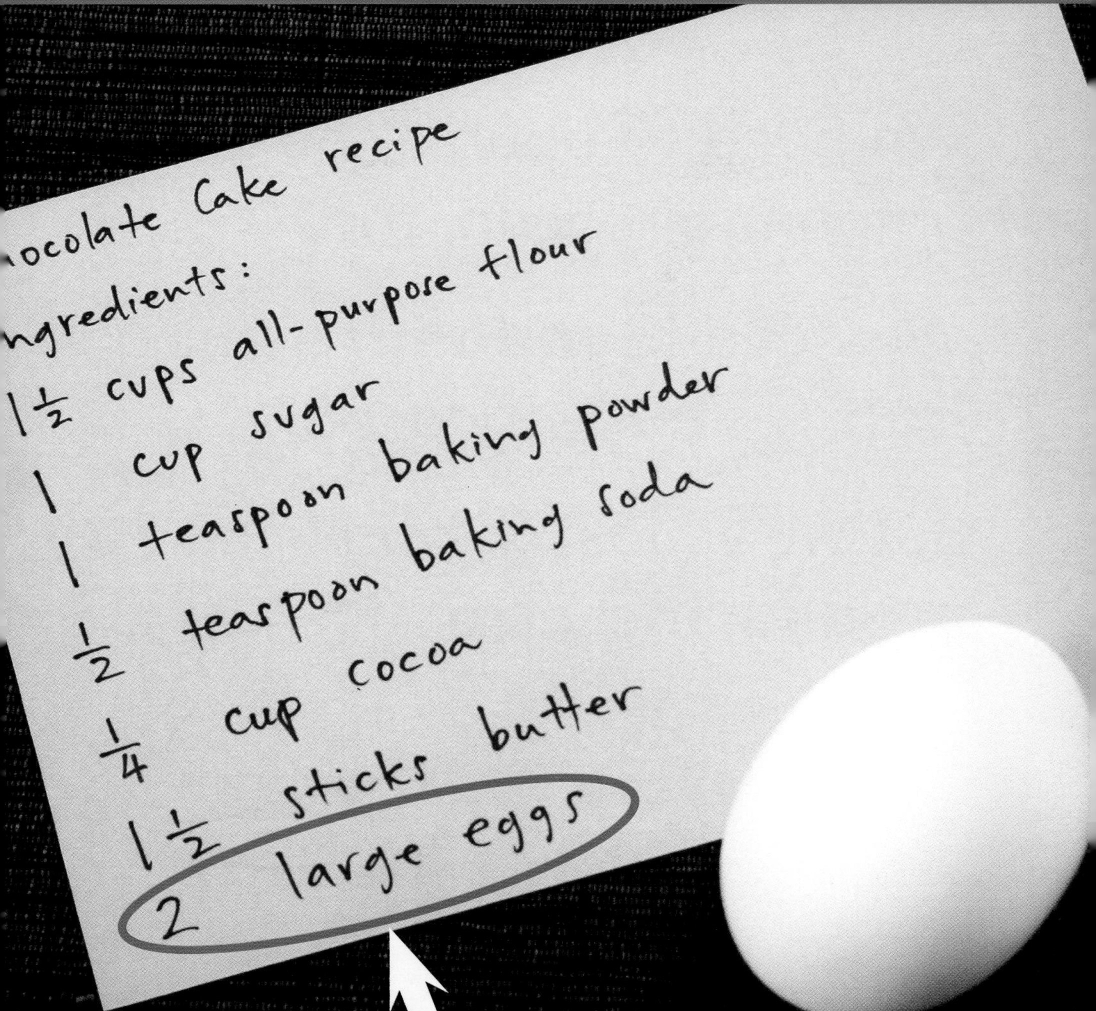

Chocolate Cake recipe

Ingredients:

1½ cups all-purpose flour

1 cup sugar

1 teaspoon baking powder

1 teaspoon baking soda

½ teaspoon cocoa

¼ cup

1½ sticks butter

2 large eggs

$$2 \times 2 = ?$$

We need to double the amount of cocoa, too.

We need to **measure** out a **half** ($\frac{1}{2}$) **cup** of cocoa.

But we've lost the half-cup **measuring cup**!

measure

No worries. We can use the **quarter** $\left(\frac{1}{4}\right)$ **cup** instead.

We need a half cup of cocoa.

How many quarter cups of cocoa will equal 1 half cup of cocoa?

Turn to page 23 for the answer.

$\frac{1}{4}$ cup + $\frac{1}{4}$ cup = $\frac{1}{2}$ cup

Now it's time to make the frosting.

We need to melt 100 chocolate chips.

How are we going to count so many chips?

How many chocolate chips do you think are in this pile?

When we don't have time to count, we can **estimate**.

How do you estimate the number of chips?

Take a close look, think about it, and make a good guess.

Which pile has close to 100 chips?

Turn to page 23 for the answer.

Which pile do you think has close to 100 chips in it?

The cake came out looking great!

We cut 6 pieces on one side.

We'll do the same on the other side.

Will all 12 of us get enough cake?

Turn to page 23 for the answer.

YOUR NEW WORDS

estimate (**es**-tuh-mate) to make a guess about the approximate size or cost of something

half cup (haf kup) a measurement equal to half of one cup

measure (**meh**-zhur) to figure out how long, wide, deep, or heavy something is

measuring cup (**meh**-zhu-ring kup) a tool used when cooking to measure out exact amounts of ingredients

multiply (**muhl**-tuh-ply) to add the same number to itself several times

quarter cup (**kwor**-tur kup) a measurement equal to one-fourth of one cup

recipe (**res**-uh-pee) instructions for preparing and cooking food

Page 10

To double something, you can multiply it by 2. The recipe calls for 2 eggs.

2 x 2 = 4 You need 4 eggs.

Page 14

To double something, you can also add the number to itself.

$\frac{1}{4} + \frac{1}{4} = \frac{2}{4} = \frac{1}{2}$

You need 2 quarter-cups of cocoa.

Page 18

The first pile has 10 chips in it. If you compare that pile to the other 2 piles, you can estimate which pile has 100 chips.

The pile on the right has 100 chips.

Page 20

The cake is cut into 2 equal parts, or halves. Each half is cut into 6 pieces.

6 + 6 = 12 Yes, all 12 people will get a piece of cake.

INDEX

FIND OUT MORE

Book:
Mattern, Joanne. *I Use Math in the Kitchen*. Milwaukee, WI: Weekly Reader Early Learning Library, 2006.

Website:
PBS Kids: Games Central—Can You Fill It?
http://pbskids.org/cyberchase/games/liquidvolume/

MEET THE AUTHOR
Ellen Weiss has received many awards for her books for kids. She lived in England for a short time, where people say "maths" instead of "math."